PRAISE FOR *COUNTLESS CINEMAS*

"Michael McLaughlin writes poetry like a West Coast abstract painter on film. Like Diebenkorn, his work captures California light—the soft seductive light of ocean and ochre hills—and then he uses that light to illuminate the deep, often pitch black, interior thoughts of a range of characters from youthful rebels to long-haul drivers, even the mother of a suicide bomber. But these are not still lives. In McLaughlin's highly-charged collection, scenes are meshed and viewed in motion: the start/stop of an L.A. freeway at rush hour where tension builds as thoughts explode from station to station; the long sweep of a 100 mph drive on four-lane north-south interstate highways where images drift by dreamlike in a fluid, changing landscape. From his perch on California's Central Coast, McLaughlin unleashes the true ecstatic nature of the state, in poems that drift from cities to mountains to maximum security forensic facilities like Atascadero State Hospital, where he has been artist-in-residence for more than 20 years. Man Ray, to whom he devotes a poem, called California 'a beautiful prison.' In *Countless Cinemas*, McLaughlin opens the prison gates and shows us California from a fresh, imaginative, troubling, and deeply personal perspective. Roll film."
—Kat Georges, Editor-in-Chief, Three Rooms Press; Poet, *Our Lady of the Hunger*

"Michael McLaughlin chronicles the unconventional, even transgressive experiences and points of view we all have but rarely reveal to others. Syntactically inventive and imagistically daring, his poems invite us to confront events from the past and present in order to understand the way we keep these events private and thus free of public shame. McLaughlin is a poet of the exposed, unvarnished realities of the human psyche."
—Kevin Clark, PhD, CSU San Luis Obispo, *Self-Portrait with Expletives, In the Evening of No Warning, The Mind's Eye: A Guide to Writing Poetry*

COUNTLESS CINEMAS

COUNTLESS CINEMAS

by Michael McLaughlin

HELL PRESS
UNIVERSITY OF HELL PRESS

This book published by University of Hell Press.
www.universityofhellpress.com

© 2016 Michael McLaughlin

Book Design by Vince Norris
www.norrisportfolio.com

Cover Artwork by Arthur Taussig
www.arthurtaussig.com

Published in the United States of America.
ISBN 978-1-938753-19-0

To Dona—my end all and be all

"He who sought to escape the world becomes its translator, too. Who can escape? The container is closed."

—Henri Michaux, Preface to Elsewhere

TABLE OF CONTENTS

Railing Too Cold I Want To Stop

the drug of morning and the
drug of fall come forward
in the stunted marigold drag blonde
lobelia of dawn
                    these success flowers

have no faces
whether singular or clumped
brown subways snail tanker and slug
they are the leaf hoppers finger crushed
earwig grumpy
crocodile sow bug scuttling
rafts of searing pain
fungus neighbors by the name each
sun grows shorter

(not the shine), I connect to people
blight or rust who've died

I've loved the railing too cold I want to stop.

The Avenal State Prison & Larry Rivers Died Draft Two Blues

Avenal State Prison, Avenal, California

The white number 70 Larry Rivers stencil
Me running Late On 46.
The white number 70 Larry Rivers stencil
Me running Late On 46.
A speeding ticket
With my workshop At seven.
Should've known there'd be some kind of hitch.

Cop gone, ninety a hundred, maybe that will save the day
Cop gone, ninety a hundred, maybe that will save the day
Tumble weed, piled up stubble,
Barbwire   They call hay.

Plastic chair, styrofoam cooler,
three hubcaps 'gainst a ditch
Plastic chair, styrofoam cooler,
three hubcaps 'gainst a ditch.
Jet plume snaky
turquoise; the foothills.
Pink flaked particulate.

The joint's lit up
like a bathroom
Every bit of it.
The joint's lit up
like a bathroom
Every bit of it.
Doesn't matter

what size the dinner.
I wouldn't risk taking a shit.

Tomato onion Bear Claw chlorine
Yard Four, where they live.
Tomato onion Bear Claw chlorine
Yard Four, where they live.
Next time you pass one of the homeless
Make that instant. Of your life. Their gift.

Sonny Kurt Enrique Jamie
Forcellini.
Neihart Lamb.

Sonny Kurt Enrique Jamie
Forcellini.
Neihart Lamb.

You wouldn't 've kept coming
'Cept it hooked you.

Now you know.
Poetry's
No Hallmark scam.

Summer Eve South of Stockton

One hundred well-behaved right lane trucks.
Fast Lane I-5. Eighty mile per hour
twilight toasting the minds of bugs.
Phone pole hawk. Beak tucked.
Crop duster Christmas time green. Envying
the guy whose first kiss must
have just taken hold in rich rye
of such an instant just passed.

Ah, the heat of it! We're no more than bread!

Back seat my son, you'd think
Asleep on
the upholstery of heaven.

For an instant so righteous
I'm entrusted with so much.

Night's just a nest
my job's just to drive
for an instant so righteous.

Daylight Savings Time / de Kooning

Art never seems to make me peaceful or pure.
I always seem to be wrapped in the melodrama of vulgarity.

— Willem de Kooning

I

The clock says it's nine o'clock
but it's really eight o'clock,
if it's fall.

It's very difficult for a painter
to be free of the material.

I rip open the salami
in fear of someone waking up.

Just as I reach the desk
I have to take a piss

It's very difficult for a painter
to be free of the material

A frozen glimpse; swiss cheese,
a fig

not so much this particular glimpse,
but the emotion of it

that's the hardest thing, not to reason
but *to be* a rock somewhere.

the clock says it's nine o'clock
but it's really eight o'clock,
if it's fall.

II

I'm a housepainter who gets very excited
every once in awhile

four bottles   the color of sunrise
windows
with a little green

one thing about space, it just keeps going.

when you want to cross a street in busy traffic
you have to fill it up very fast

an innocence about nature is needed
if you want to break up space

when I'm out on the beam a little when I'm slipping, I say
hmmmn, this is very interesting.

When I'm falling
I'm doing alright

it's really a wonderful sensation
to slip into this glimpse

when I'm standing upright, I'm stiff

I want to grasp the abstract
and that's really the most difficult thing.

Dear Steven

Today I heard you died six months ago.
Charley told me he'd run into Lorraine
That book fair.
Westwood.
You know the one.

You didn't think it'd get you.
Bad flu. Growing stronger.
Pneumonia.
Later.
Long time positive. HIV.

You did it.
Sold your first novel
Remember the party, I do.
Beat of the tom-tom.
Terry MacMillan, Vanessa Williams *A Soldier's Story*,
The principles. Your long-time paramour.
Then also positive. How you loved Sting.
More for his looks than his music
I always thought. *No Easy Place to Be*
Someday up on "the Carson"
even Arsenio You'd said. I
could care less about tv
You didn't seem seriously black enough, somehow
But what should black enough seriously be?

We lit up often, I didn't mind You
thinking I was cute, funny

Most sensitive white boyman you ever knew.
Often. Literally.
Dear in London likened
to Jimmy Baldwin
like your Jewish agent
Maybe Even Actually Said.
And sometimes I was around
You know I knew
To make some new white lover jealous
Who doesn't ever use color or sex?

Serious enough You were the only one. Real
enough, "If you had to choose
between your writing and your wife which would you give up?"
you asked.
Those kinds of questions.
— My wife. I said

And six years later Me
my verdant saltine soft California ocean countryside You live
2nd street. NYC. Marriage kaput. So it went.
She said to me, you don't have a conventional
bone in your body.
That's just what I love 'bout you, brother.
Busting up. 'Woman put it perfectly.'

Then Third novel tour
Blond Quebecois Banker boy New lover My advice
You solicited. What is about you and these Aryans, man?
Blonds in dusters on Fifth Avenue and shit?

Such Times firing up,
Phone crazed for hours.
Shared histrionics Faded fools
faux incensed.

You were in Baltimore The Mexican lover
Thrown food   His family More thrown food
His Bedside snits. Seizures. Fits.
His last seven weeks, the Chronic Oh Zee I sent.

Good comrade Derek knew you died four months ago
I called the assbite each week for two months. He has yet
to call me back.
Bastard. Why do we have to find out
This way? Why?
How your respect
For my work Still uplifts
me. Though
Where to go with it?

I left a message on my ex's voicemail
But Fuck if
she bothered to respond

She and I having to leave
Your birthday party Early
Too many black people
She so disconcerted
And me so.
Freaking ashamed.

I went to your thirty-fourth birthday—a much better
time—alone.
Enjoyed your friends spanked on steroids—
if only they'd been women
Hitting on—Nah.
I would've reigned it in.

One of the few artists I'd ever felt tight with.
That mother of a SoCal anthology
That fuzz nut statue of Tommy Trojan
Your galactic generosity of spirit.
Who knows what might have been?

Country Drive

A scar between headaches raises
the road's wrong vein. A piece of tongue
on the moon
a stray arrow.

Heard the sun at night?

The trees have legs like dogs,
like dogs
the stars
freeze a whisper
in the rear view mirror.

The Dump

Menlo Park, California 1963

Here in the '61 Ford Ranchero, shale silica king of ships.
Burlap sack subdued rusty ski chain. Three-in-One cement tire
tetherball stand. Pickleweed. A heron. Off Bayshore. Egg stink old
shoe Bulldozer pants. Nothing better than riding in the bed.

As the guy's on the wall phone, Dad works a dime over.
Every knuckle and back. Peter Lorre style flies get thick. Your
grandfather got the Ranchero to move pianos, he yells. After he
bought the Warehouse from Bekins.   Back in Klamath Falls, he
adds.

A fist some dollar bills, by the square yard. Plywood sugar
shack. Shouldn't be standing up in the bed like that, kid. Yellow
jackets. Marlon Perkins. Muskrat dens. Mutual of Omaha's *Wild
Kingdom*. Smoke under the No Smoking sign. Not until the station
wagon goes can we get in. This sixth grade kid showed us how to
rub pennies. In the snack machine, you get potato chips.

Sunset. House Beautiful. Fortune. What do you want to
do crown someone, as my magazines flop over the side. Wait until
I get the tailgate. Two by fours, toyon, madrone, the old cabinet
doors. One of Amy's dolls. I snuck a box of your mother's pine
cones in, don't tell her. Can we stop and play mini golf at the
Windmill? War of the Worlds. Seagulls dip and soar. Open Sunday,
the new sign says.

Your mother's making her scalloped potatoes. I need you
to help barbecue the flank steak. How fast can you sweep out that
bed?

I'm old enough, you say, not to fall out rusty stingray, tire
flat, yellow fridge. Hydrangea, old lady petticoat washing machine,
open door filmstrip kids don't lock your fourth grade safety in.

Suffocate. Duck and Cover Sputnik lawn mower. Dichondra clipping drifts. Space race, Hills Brothers coffee, head for the hills, white robes, covered heads. Marichal, McCovey, Mays, the San Fran Chronicle Sporting Green. Tailgate slam. All set? Prickers, bottle cap, Lemon Pledge, smashed carnation. Use your teeth instead.

You get tears from the wind and it's freezing but nothing's better than when you go this fast.

You squish pyracantha berries and they're yellow. Christmas robins, according to dad. Like they've been drinking under the mistletoe. It's fun to watch them try and land.

I Had a Better Poem to Read

At my mom's memorial service
at Christ Church Episcopal
Portola Valley.
I was about to read a poem.
Then I remembered the only time we'd cried together.

The Park Theater, Menlo Park.
She'd taken me to *To Die in Madrid*.

To Die in Madrid was about the Spanish Civil War.
She'd taken me out of school to see it. She'd never
been a mom like that.

I wanted to share this moment
with the gathering
but had a better poem to read.

Not about how she'd
battled Alzheimer's for ten years
as if every day was her Battle of Brunette,
every breakfast a crawl up Normandy beach.

I had a better poem to read.
No silhouette of a German Heinkel bomber
like the model I'd made in sixth grade.
Nor the Soviet T-26 tank by a cathedral gate.
No Hemingway trying to horn in or
Garcia Lorca
facing the firing squad.

Bodies in piles, sliding over each other
pushed by a bulldozer's blades.

Nothing about how she'd swept
a breakfast bowl of Valencia oranges
onto the floor. Sobbing.
Then screaming.

A few weeks earlier.

Declarative Parts of Speech Poetic Americana Bill of Rights

Freedom to coronate each and any pauper noun a proper noun.

Freedom to coronate each and any paragraph blundering in wunderkind, stanzas of disunified thought.

Freedom to endow articles with prepositional knighthood, bestow prepositions ultimate articledom.

Freedom to singularize plurals and misquotate all reported speech.

Freedom to conjunctivate all action words, verb all the adverbtised singularities plurally to bed.

Freedom to kind color number any object's prepositional resistance transfusion interjection like.

Freedom to facet all high syntax into unwieldy weddings ring.

Gravity for Agnostics

after Emily Dickinson

True us in a manner
Keep us green

As if finding in
Sun's taste

Some face.

Apt.   As morning is.

Today's Death

for David Hirschman, Leukemia

The sun skirmishes with a shadow
As today's death commences
in the ointment
of a word. On the rug

A broken bird's song. In the air
a plane's business,
stretching beyond the last palm.

To go afield

in the batcavelime of body, a continent of
minutes meander like amoeba, to go places you
want to go, a brown short summer
fizzles above your face, to go

chic in the red beret you wear, David, or
hip in a longshoreman's
knit, baseball cap
gap smile or still
another sudden hat, I thought the fabric, and

the color bursting each day, a
small dark flower. This
morning

at a place nearby, you
suggested we go, for some coffee, so

long since Santa Cruz, since
you saw Billy in
the Cascades, or Tacoma, or
somewhere—

A girl

your sister calls.
The stars
Scatter

like thieves.

Blue Moon
to Dona

Your car   In the Blue is my heart
Your face your feet
blue of my heart street
Bounce

Joy Bird grace
All
is blue
About you

Each sunset blue tree
of my bed
Heart piercing

Each neckblue ice cream
nude Zula In hand holding kitchens
Each millrace dream
Balm Tears always blooming

I knew crying Blue full
blonde the quick
damp blue varnishing

In booms Of kitchen laundry
Blue dawned laugh Kittens

I knew then bacon nuked Iron cord
Unplugged for safety

Sweater's Full moon
Comet blue, Shorts
Too
Bright
Blue windows

Blue moment bic cigarettes
with Full moon quickness
Blue Monet Magritte newsprint
warm palm snakeblue silvers
Blue flicks in ever night
Protostar   Blue as phone line hairpins

Blue moon don't you know you are always with me

And the Star Silver mooned Redwoods
Cerulean church
blue Sadness

Joy death Helios
of heart blue dominion

Each burst   Lunar fall

Blue

All
about you

All is about you in the blue of my heart.

Neck Surgery Summer Exercise Program

Stand as shown neck
Stand as shown neck surgery
arms with blades
at sides Repeat rotating shoulders
Forward

Small movements
time per day

Repeat rotating shoulders
forward   Small   Movements
Time
Per day

Stand as shown

Shoulders downward
small
Shoulder blade
Moments
pinched in neck
as shown

Blade hold pressed
pinch shoulders downward
Stand small moments
Blade at side pinched arm shoulder blade
as shown

New Cathedrals

It looked like a deer fly
on tv. One of those
bugs that could bite hard. Horizontal
Stealth wing Bomber Black.

Metal sharp
Into the monolith
like butter. Then
into Kubrick's
other. A second one.

What else but erect new cathedrals
If vaporized, imploded
Assemble more?

People dribbling out of windows
Like swans of burnt
Plastic. People
          Dropping.
          Holding hands.

Allstate First Liberty Delta
Morgan Stanley Metropolitan Life

And then ash,
computer disc expense report memos
Body parts. All over the place

I had to pull over the car and cry

It sounded like when you have a bunch
of spaghetti and you break it in half

to boil

Paralyzed by the smell
of jet fuel building

Flocks
of paper lost.
Shuffling.
Separate the sky

Finally we ran for it. This guy we were
talking to saw at least twelve
people jump out of the building
One tried to shimmy
Down the outside
slipped.

Figures ripped at my shirt
tried to
get my flashlight
Their skin gray
Shamble
Footstep smoky stairs

people slag sucked out
of desk chair
windows Rain
on Avenues below

One man, but he didn't grab her fast enough
Suddenly realized he was holding
just an arm

Tens of thousands of people grimy, marching
Northward, away
I just wanted to find my kids and my
wife and get the hell off this island.
As if the pilot'd had
The throttle
completely floored.

Black for dead, red immediately
life threatening
Serious yellow
Walking.
Coded green

Tourists bustling into the White House
While others absconded
(So many blood donors
Bellevue no more bags)
With their lives

Four Czechs at the Empire State
building Bought up
all the World Trade Center pictures.

"Soon no more
These cards, also." One explained.

What else but build new cathedrals.
Consecrate still more.

I Don't Know

Jalal and I worked in the Shack's Ft Worth warehouse.
Where neither of us wanted to be.

Both our families were military.
Purple birds, golden eagles
Death in the name of a belief system
Be all that you can be.
Big fun ordering pitchers at Tumbleweeds
Though he believed in blasphemy

Over Marlboros, we talked books, religion, family
Baghdad, Damascus, Jerusalem
Istanbul, Rome and Greece.

How the Romans fashioned living torches
out of Jews and Christians. How
to bring libraries to the after life,
An Egyptian's mummy would be wound up
In the poetry of Greece.

The Crusades, I told Jalal were about jihading Catholics
trying to overrun Jerusalem. Their lion-hearted version
of a safari, like some Middle Ages Macy's parade.

I very much like Gandhi but I am Muslim, he explained.

Level with me, man. Is all the Sunni, Shia
brouhaha as messed up as I believe?
The bloodline of the prophet versus the succession of caliphs?

Pretty much so, man, he said.

Irish Protestant and Italian Catholic.
My grandparents. So scandalous
their parents would never speak.

Moslems and Hindus, Hindus and Buddhists
Is to die for *the same* as to kill for?
Power, faith and violence.

Yes, that is true. Power.
But I am Sunni, he smiled, *all the same.*
Just as you told me you were Christian, all the same.

I was just trying to make a point, you misunderstood me.
Christian was the way I was raised.

Same. One cannot break up with the way he's raised.

I had Jalal's family over once
He mine. Me.

Our wives distrusted our friendship.
Bonded over
our camaraderie.

Why is this, he asked
Our better halves, I whispered. *Spies for the CIA.*

Jalal liked the phrase, Search me.

One day he disappeared.
No response my dispatches.
Raps on his door not a peep.

Why you so interested in that raghead?
A co-worker accosted me.

A phone call shit finally. *First, Jim,*
I cannot meet you.
Remember the day you were sick?

Do I ever. 9/11. 24/7, my wife
Glued to the freakin' screen.

Well, when I clocked in for work, that 11ᵗʰ day
Took my coffee. Went to get my gloves.

Uh-huh.

I asked Tim what he needed.
He said to finish with the pallets
So I started to work. So, I work twenty minutes
half an hour and he says, Enough. Enough is enough. Go home
Why? I said.
You're Arabic, isn't it obvious?
You didn't hear about New York and Washington?
You didn't see how many of our people your people killed?

I didn't do nothing. I told him.

Anything.

*Yes, anything. I work here. I said. Longer than you. Texas
is my home.*

*Then Tim says Go pray in your mosque.
Go pray with your leader. We don't want you around.*

At first, I think this is a joke. You know how that big guy is.

A horse's ass. Just as he's always been.

*So come here. He says. I want to show you something. In his office,
He has a gun.*

*So I went home. Told Ahlam, to tell Hala, tell the boys. We have to
leave.
I had my check coming but I didn't go back.
No way, Jose.*

Whoa, whoa, whoa, Jalal.
Remember when Ahlam
Was in the labor? Payroll let me sign for you then.
I'll get it. You earned that money. We just need to meet afterwards.

*Jim, Tim knows my address
I need a gun. I have my family to protect.*

Protect?

The Man Ray Story

To create is divine, to reproduce human.
—Man Ray

Lips were a flag for bodies
many people flew at once.

California was a beautiful prison
Movement and sexual tension
—I'm sure it's the same way now.

I was of my time, simple.

If you explain the woman crossing the street
I'll explain the object of myself.

Remembrance

I cried today
for Samir Ammar Al Masani
killed on Via Dolorosa
in Jerusalem.

The traditional route: Jesus' crucifixion.
Why are they killing
these teenage kids?

Guns in hand soldiers sit
on Palestinian roofs
God's chosen, the Israelis
They've got their fucking land.

I cried the pool of blood
his body left
Troops firing on Muslims
Leaving their prayers.
Friends dipping their hands
in the blood from his head.

I cried for my son whose blood is yours.
My family, my friends whose blood
is yours.

I cried my tiny pool of hopeless defiance.
As the red hands
of Samir's friends were held aloft

I cried for those kids. All kids.
Our kids.

As his friends took their hands.
　　　　Stone walls of the alley. Prints
　　　　lining
　　　　the walls
　　　　In remembrance.

Trains

San Luis Obispo, California

when i moved here from big city trains
were in the hills
night fucking angels
sucking braking metal root reaching
where the we as ice plant
keeping me had gone

go-tired frog chorus chorus
eucalyptus
frog chorus of have you cum

so that when *you* left for your
twenty-four count child molester
i had to warfare blind angry children
tomato seed inane-eyed small town cop

i won the understanding of idiot's arm
around the moon bright scaffolding
full physical   legal of my son

and he was four that we would walk
the tracks stolen radio
bourbon angel iron the moist
blood
and run

and i would smash inside
your jehovah's witness rocks at cars   come

swaying fat i would shoot
you   come

coupling and uncoupling
trees some driver's side swung open
to fornicate two teenagers

in a mini van shooting crows
were i to go to the pen (what i wouldn't do)
my boy wouldn't
have a dad
                    what i wouldn't do

to avoid
having to kill.

Love Is a Stillness

I'm writing with the woman who lies inside
of me
Who tastes of railroad tracks
and though I can make her nearly anytime
I want,
I enter nowhere.
I enter a nowhere with cosmetics
Instead of shaving cream.
I enter nightgowns instead
of jockey shorts, dresses in lieu of
jeans, I enter dreams which
are much more barren and when
I think I'm entering the body
of a needy person who's doing
her best, that I can comfort and
fuck and help, I long to
lie with the man inside The man
who's helping me write this Now.
Kid man who always wanted to be
A star athlete for the love and
adulation despite the emptiness
skill, mastery
if, for no other
reason, but
for love.

I'm lying now with the man who knows
this face, these shoulders, these arms
this cock This head so much better

than the woman inside
Were this woman on the outs, she'd have
me. Always has
Pouting, insouciant. Hard to pin down. Lost
My body'd rear up follow thought

Gear. Wisdoms
of its own.

Wheeling, rearing, forgiveness.
Pacing.
Reluctant in retreat.

And I'd think body, how could you be so wrong?
Love is a stillness. Self-contained.

Attack of the Fifty-Foot Costa Rican

On the Trans American Highway in Costa Rica
we nearly hit a guy
Drunk, lunging cross our lane
south of Puntarenas.

After seeing my first flight of macaws.
Just north of crocodile bridge.

Killing some fool in another country
what a drag that would have been.
What made me recall it?

People as termites?
Colonizing insects?
Legions of dullards as Dostoyevsky said?

Say you were two hundred feet
Tall looking down
like in that *Twilight Zone*. Spacesuit guys
with bubble heads.

Warring against the ant world, for example.

How totally they would outnumber us.
They'd be a hundred times stronger.
We with our brains. And bombs and stinging
guns. Still, they'd mandible us to death.

Hell, imagine the fifty-foot woman

what if she decided to give you head?

Hopeless as a King Kong bi-plane
or just a spitwad 'neath her alien web.

Fruitless to scream! And beg for death!

I'm glad we missed that joker in Costa Rica.
Not hitting him was heaven sent.

With Me That Night Scared

My five year old got into bed with me.
Scared of you.

I'd like to think.

You, a twenty-eight count, down for twelve year child molester,
Two daughters (every orifice) daddy games.

You, a twenty-eight count violation of trust pedophile
who my ex thought she could make parole better for
by having the kid around.

You the fat fuck I wanted to dice up chop up
Dump into the ocean, fifteen miles off
off Avila, dinner for the big white there.

You, the man she's now living with.

That night, I found you
in a house of shower curtains.

Curtains please. The dream begins.

You'd come over with my ex.
Both of you in my bedroom. Talking.
She didn't make sense.

No longer
did she have a stomach Just

a pelvic bone and ribs.
She was naked on the bed
I said, *Thinner than ever. You* got mad.
I recognized her foot. *Put on this*, you said,
holding up a red teddy, *I want to suck you why*
don't you join us?

You were the walrus among his oysters
I didn't know how to kill yet, so I went
Into another room. Your daughter, the one you butt fucked
The eight year old who had you in her mouth. She wasn't there
I didn't see her
but her pearly fingers were yours.

Then I was alone at night knew you were coming back turned out
the light.
Waiting to face you, window unlatched.
I saw your silhouette through the shower glass my kitchen
Didn't have no weapon. Heard you
Breathing through your mouth
Said, *What the fuck you doing here?*
You just smiled. Said, *I'm gonna nail your ass.*

I led you out the front door as you listened.
Easy as pie to lead.
(Wouldn't, couldn't kill you
Just the be-with-it Being bigger
than both of us)
Said, *Your ass'll be in some hole forever, you come back.*

Then *you* started screaming

Saying that *I* had made *your* life hell
Saying it could never be worse.

Pulling at my wrist
You ran past me into a pile of garbage
Which burst into flames.

Burning away into a bigger pile,
I could hear you scream. Could only see your feet
As you infernoed on the four poster bed.

I couldn't bring myself to save you.
And could only watch with the same fear I'd had
When you'd broken into my house.

Toys, gifts and
touch-me-theres
beneath the big top house of mirrors

There was a child on my lap, Filipino, I think, I didn't
Notice her eyes. *You're not like the others,* she said.
You're the different one.

And I knew
I could only kill you
by leading you into different rooms.

A taste of your own medicine.
This being how you worked.

Love by Power

A steel smell is what the clouds have   In
advertisements of rain
Chameleon green
Those I work with.
Meal after meal
Deranged Rocked up Psychotic
Incarcerated
Unbound
My five year old son makes for love When
he gets into my bed. We measure love by power
and violence as most men
big Or little do Orange canopy
after comforter Each
tent above our head.
Chinese white cover sheet We're safe
What wrestles gentle in our
Valor Triumph The boymind We killed them,
Captain. It feels so good
to get them dead.
You gotta flash your sword around a woman
If you wanta hurt a guy, get him here
Battle after battle before him
Armies
so Easy
to dispense, dismiss.

Leaning on my elbow
His epic.
I listen his world away in graves. A Maginot Line

the Jerries have yet to storm
Hannibal, Charlemagne, The X-men
Ghengis Khan, Alexander the Great
Bent bodies, head to elbow
Wrestling
Cracking necks
sunlanced to spring Woozy shadows
Burrowing back he wants to stay
in bed
The world closing beyond our bulwark
Is chrome. Calendar schemes
to-do list notions All named
Tomorrow Acquaintances Paint
Plastic Empty heads.
And as I return from his kindergarten drop off Every
nightbook That we've ever read I burn through another day
gird myself
For what feels so dear.
The world's poison is
Always so near.

Whatever the world can't poison
I hug
Close as possible to my chest.

Canto XI from The Book of Divorce

It's pay a bill make five phone calls have
a thought die
Pay a bill have five phone thoughts make
a call die
Drive to die make a store house have a phone
child sigh
Make a call have five phone bills drive to
store die
Sigh a phone child eat a bill make a
springtime cry
Cry a paycheck read a bill eat some
crying pay
Make a color color a call smile a smile
eat
Phone a smile fake a paycheck color
son's phone bath bathe
Bash the laundry phone a bed sheet wish a phone girl
ball
Bill a number bind the newsprint smell
some flowers cry
Gas the car up bill the cat food vacuum two
flea thoughts eat
Call the sunset bill a moonrise pace the
kitchen   Breathe.

No End

My body felt the same weakness

                                    everything.

Just like yesterday.

Only this was a year ago.

Shot in the head
my Devin
as he drove down a residential street.

He'd hold a hand
to his mouth when he laughed
to cover that crooked tooth.

He'd been so chubby as a child;
baseball cards, comic books
collecting. As soon as he
could read.

As a teenager he seemed
to grow tall
            lankyovernight

Hair styled, shirts matching his shoes,
always groomed. His friends
calling him Pretty Boy.

He was shy, always
hanging back, letting all the others

hold court.
When he went to a club with his friends,
he'd lounge along the wall
refuse to dance.

He was going to City College then.
Wanted to be a police officer
he said

I'd just bought him
the white Monte Carlo.

He was so proud
of those new rims.

The night he was shot
he was driving to his girlfriend's.
Crashed into the Thomases' garage

The neighbors heard him try
to restart the car.

That's where he died,
they said.

Smoke Shop Soledad

*Nothing has really happened unless it's been
explained.*   —Virginia Woolf

Gandalf drifts
along the bulwark
from one row of bongs
to the next.

Bong bong
Laser strobe
Big Ben.

I marvel at the black light Chief Joseph
Flash on my San Luis Obispo
Syrian liquor store friend.

Ke Fack, How are you?
Ahlan wa sahlan.
Good   Taman.

What up, stirs Gandalf
of the wispy beard.

What it is.

The Moody Blues, I think
Early '70s. Pasco, Washington. First girlfriend

The pierced nipple.

Festering in Portland.
Stale service station
Larks and Carltons

Then curling in the window
Marilyn

In her egg white
updraft dress.

Special today
on our electronics.

Electric cigarettes.

Boardwalk

Santa Cruz, California, 1976

Candyland too real to be crazy true, seated on two-toned
bench playing old man alone paint sky blue Continental drift band
saw   On bandstand Horizons

Oh sand, sand, the no-fault sand, milkshake blast shadow,
aggregate arm foundations Shadow of time, of blackbird, of
scavenger gull

Shadow of sparrow hunting for popcorn Coast Guard chopper
postage stamp
white sardine shadow   Star striped unflappable over Fritz
Langed white building

Bank vault filing cabinet food scrappers sky Fog which
strangely isn't dropping isn't waxing round the motels and date
palm fly-by cyclists

Tug of paisley pink dress, pouch of Disneyland t-shirt
Rolls of florid gingham home-cooked U.S. Grade A fat. Kid
warm, mother warm, father dry checked pants warm

Deep burrowing kisses, warm against the rail, sweater
barefoot chipped nail polish Ideal Fish warm, filmy floral
shift capri neon clam chowder warm Warm, eating warm,
clinging Woolworth-close warm   Sitting beer bagged for
low profile warm.

His mouth is dry-stretched like an old tuna's
Khaki golf cap Silverado Country Club retired   Sunglasses
Sidewalks   Crack
Acres for miles   Tic tac toes off his shoes to pick at his
feet   Small mouth   The freeze dried expressions of
the old   Custodial zip jacket, navy blue cotton pants paper into
back pocket, finished, folded stiff where he leans, he walks, legs

crowbarred by age

So it's in his hands the thin man from Dublin, ex miner, slug nose, resting on a shoulder-sand-blasted Anglo, so it's in his hands

Boats with their knitting needle masts a-sway, sea rustling, Irish Setters, slow parade of campers, station wagons, vans, *What timedoya got*, my brother-in-law sez, ice cream low slung tinkle bell blues

Cellophane and louder, unlaced kids, paper bags, whoosh of gull, Glad bag ham sandwich, pigeon bread crust Birkenstock, Adidas and louder, four-inch fire engine soles clang grinding past the bench, longhair grease shuffle, oil of cotton candy, malt liquored sideburns, the half-mast eyes, knives, chains winding, sharp macho amusement Chicana, don't touch, she dishes herself out, stare so copper fat bronzed that a Stroller tips over

Beneath the looks, sly and shy, slimy rocks boarded over, an ocean's lips lick and play

So I followed the thin # 2 Pencil Man, most variety now in the faces, the faces, rides running—no more than two or three people brothers blaring Herbie/Grover, honk-polished mono sax from a black attaché forty pound cassettea dad points out rides, family tribes, resemblances blue Bermuda kneecaps, a blue-zigged white shirt, a dangling Minolta, head and butt hanging out, white socks with black loafers, green-tinted sunglasses, a smile like Roosevelt's, tickets twenty-five cents

So I followed the # 2 Pencil Man past the animal-pitch-dime-on-top-dish wins and the orange-yellow groundswell screams and Spanish, past the Forty-Niner game, macro scree ball jeans pumping, losing sight of the Dubliner, past fast service walkup window eatoutoceanview, we got tables on the pavement with its alltimesummer spill, three throws, the cat rack, oneinyouwin

fascination, fifty cents, three rolls for a quarter dip-top cones,
Diana Ross transvestites   Take available horse, where had he
gone?

Under the bumper car minimum height requirement,
wienerschnitzel cops, pizza-pasta-a-beer, another coin toss perhaps,
indoor golf, pokerino

Indoor glimpse, indoor warm, indoor nicotine splash,
sammyhitshot, lovepilot, crook's saloon, motorama, upper deck,
periscope, the lord's prayer—a welcome gift—stunt cycle, electric
eye, four-star subtank

He had disappeared into the coalminer's sky, no Mr.
Clean, that mop won't do

Open alley   Benny Good Man
Secret ways of blinking
You must think this is where Santa Cruz started.

Homeless in Hollywood
to Todd

Torn cloud tired is the semen sky.

Between which clotheslines burn
his women. In blurs
Of eggbeater palm. His women who testify
with lowered snout, clicking paw and sharpened frond.
Who testify every morning will bring more night.

We're your Birds of Paradise, his women exclaim.
Your Christmas cacti, they whisper. *Your spindly pine*.

As astride a white enamel whirlpool gate,
he wavers, hops
before noting—unlocked.
Washes his socks. Dries them on the fence,
after most tenants have left
For work. Uncorks himself. Then studies his shirt.

Mr No Say, a gardener with his own pick-up truck
Says nothing as later, he knows, the raccoon man will
Cull what he can from dumpster piles and alley bins just
To make the ivy carpet and stunted jacaranda wall
Around his Hollywood Freeway on-ramp abode,
blocks away, more inviting.

Remember? Just that sliver?
Nineteen? Free?
Vagabond? Wannabe?

Remember dragging our backpacks up
that overpass slope in '73? I-40 to Flagstaff,
eight-thirty pm or so. Only spot where a longhair hitchin' through
Kingman might be safe, *I'd let you stay't my place, but—*
said the pinto man. After a few pipe hits apiece
Stop 'n Saturday night pickups. Beer bottles
exploding like grenades. How we'd scampered up.
Fear of rolling off the shelf, down loud cement to a Ford Ranchero death
having kept me awake. Spring had ripped its way

Through the land like a mountain range
from Tucson to Eugene. With the hobo terrier who'd
climb chain link fences on command or careening on reds,
with blue hibiscus girls, the hot station wagon ride.
Driving midnight to Mt Shasta. Dawn to
Dunsmuir and back. Divorcees, who knew? Up Zona's 17,
whining as we shot through sand cloud banks
temperature drop of true plateau.
Out of Phoenix, a Navaho pick-up, snow.
On the ground stiff thin blankets more weed behind the cab.

Reminds me of America where the beef jerky man, Needles was it?
Offered us a hitch in his borax mine jus' fordy mile
From town. Quick ink of another storm
four shotguns on the rack, as such, no, we'd said.
Later again, no, between boxcars to that worse-than-t-bird wine.
On abandoned Beaumont tracks.
Scored by shafts of light, how road moments cut,
Shrank tiny towns

Even smaller. How
Forty years ago to abandon one's skin
Fast talk could pay as it did
for our fearlessness. Reminds me of a country once
where trust was no sin.
Forty years ago. The homeless guy having left.
Such is spring. We couldn't have
traveled much further.

Kites

I remember flying kites as a kid; seven years old,
the huge field Woodside High School.
Mom didn't mind. Maybe didn't know.
I went alone.

I remember when my best friend's dad died
eating peanut butter on Saltine crackers. I want to say he deserved
it,
because he always yelled at Jimmy,
but I don't know. He was just a fatso in a flannel shirt
younger than I am now.
My other best friend in second grade, Jerry, had
an alcoholic dad. Jerry made us rum chocolate milkshakes
I didn't get sick but I took off my clothes.

When my wife gives our cats catnip and starts laughing
I think, that's what Jerry's dad did to us.
He thought I was funny staggering about,
Singing Frere Jaqua, in my underwear.

Later Jerry and I were crawling around in the rafters of an
abandoned house.
There was a pile of comic books and *Playboys* up there.
I was sitting on the trap door reading when it fell through
it collapsed my lung, I couldn't breathe and had to go to the
emergency room.

We didn't hang out much after that.
He went to a foster home when he was eleven or something,

sixth grade, I think.
I ran into his older sister
who was Miss San Mateo county, at a tennis tournament.
She looked like one of the girls from *The Brady Bunch*.
She was being honored at a Giants' game at Candlestick.
Jerry'd gotten into heroin.

Jerry and I used to hang out in a big old burnt-out eucalyptus
stump.
He liked to set fire to his sister's clothes.
I'd go there alone after his family moved.

What I liked to do was to get my kite real high.
Let all the string out. Let it go.
And then chase it Right through people's
yards.
If someone stopped me, I'd say the string got cut.
Can we help you find it?
No.

I Would Have Taken a Cleaver

Gaza Strip, November 1995

I asked the mother of a young man
who'd blown himself up
what she would have done

if she'd known
what her son was
planning to do.

I would have taken a cleaver,
cut open my heart
and stuffed him deep inside

she said.

Then I would have sewn it up tight
to keep him safe.

Somersault

I knew a death that no one shared. Somersaulting
twelve years old, in a neighbor's pool
when my friend had gone inside
to answer a phone since his parents were at work.
I wanted to set a record—twelve forward and backward
somersaults in a row—without coming up for air.

I could cheat distance under water—fifty meters
without a breath. No thought of death alone in a ball,
speed all that was important, arms
moving in circles, like paddles
or frogging along the tiled bottom
from one end to the other
and back.

But at my friend, Mark's house
I passed out. And found
the bottom of the pool on my side. The surface
so close but so far away. This was
the death I shared with myself. The cement
wasn't scratchy but soft. Geometry was there
for a moment of color, a geometry of absence
I was never meant to use.
I shared a death with myself, shooting to the surface,
it would have been too embarrassing to have been
found dead. I shared a death with myself, my so-called friend
still on the phone.

Behind the sliding glass door

two uncapped cokes on a table. The tv was on.
He was still on the phone.

I cried quickly and went home. The other world
the one

at the bottom of the pool
had been so much softer.

Cougar

Edna Valley, Triplewide

Nude on the back deck.
Reading.
We lock.
Contact.   Stare.

Whisker clock.
Marks a Lot.
Topaz.

You
break me into
perfect trees.

Ground squirrel
pounce
neck toss
snap mouth.

Willow canopy.
Weeds.

Stoneridge I

San Luis Obispo, California

Evening is to dawn as the rocks
are flowers you are
still at work.

The lichen there in a rainbow
chia, tarweed and monkey flower.

Below
a train bottles minutes by the hour.

Minutes from maps and luggage
most will never know.

The season seems to be missing.
Dog battles spot bluejays incessantly. Serpentines.
In goat-like tongues.

I have learned not to care your overactive anger
I have learned not to care you don't trust happiness
I have learned that money is of little import killing us.

We die different deaths mine walk
every morning fruit flies.
Yours away at work.

Stoneridge II

Oatmeal of the Santa Lucia
land of many smokes

Kubla Khan
without its palaces
a far cry from the opium.

A view one turns right
gravel roads to.
Meandering up the hill.

I bring back merlin scat
à la fence post.

Bluebelly reptiles
who never learn.

Why don't we sit on the hill
and drink wine anymore?
I know we are still in love.

The Art of Driving Another Color: The Twenty-Five Hour Day

The eye is greenish brown
umber early morning
faded

All atmospheres are violet
leaving SLO
white may be the light
up the two am grade we're grinding
without which no color
can be seen

I drive I love to drive

Crumb of conversation
star spackled
anatomy toy
roadface but
if I could've traded
words for paint I would've

Orange man at height
of his powers
unknown in Europe until Marco Polo
appears with his gunny sacks
of fruit from Asia
and I drive I love to drive
Indian Yellow Green Lake Extra CHP Chrome
King City the
Salinas

Only Yellow Ochre California
river trickling
south to north

I drive
I love it, red least
refractive end of the spectrum
say red and fifty people
driving 101'd see fifty
different
versions of Geranium Lake

Were there fifty people on this freeway
there's barely one

White—
a steely drum rubbed
rainbow
dream rubbed
semi Peterbilt cab flipped
back as in the oil pan dark—
silver of a trout

Crisp skirt pre dawn
running lights, jewels

A Titan Buff Golden (if you ask me—Ochre)
Yellow Oxide
Mars Orange Brown

I see the eucalypt as Jack London

called it, with the hawk's nest
thatched on top

Since I was five
every car trip—marked it

And I drive love to drive
Amtrak, twelve suppositories
passing behind me as I leave
that silver star liner in the mud

the caged single light indigo 101 halo
tomato warehouse, north of Gonzales
which angel
bulbed that siding socket
under what underwear and when?

A landmark like the hawk's nest
I am fire and flaws
India cinnabars

Dragon blood
for Greek

Dawn cracking
lusting cracked canal
fault lines of my brain
I love to drive

Sepia the temples of Kyoto ink sacs

stringy
Shinto shrine
cuttlefish

And salt
the salty Sap Green I drive

Green surmised base, they say for frescoes
wall paintings under ashes
of Pompeii

Ah, asparagus my favorite buttered green

Loving to drive fittingly Greenfield
yellow transforms
intelligence chartreuse
shots of morning
sun

Why my love my love of you
sun-up shine,
do two colors
put one next to other—sing?

Drive I drive

Force-fed mango leaves, the yellow ancient's
sacramental Indian cow urine
those old Hanuman Elephant Indian
stamps my brother had

Oh give me mud said Delacroix
and the skin of Venus
is what I will paint you

as the moms painted turquoise numbers
kid's white t-shirts in Chualar
Burnt Umber farmworker but very very rich

And what I love to do
you know

Chiron in a limo, maybe Hermes
accompanying Orpheus
Hades
dragging back Persephone

Lamp full of linseed oil
smoke strong as diesel
soot collected
makes the truest black

Driven drive red blackbird wing
diaphanous
blue's a flute, darker blue a cello
Darker still the thunderous double bass
an organ being darkest—just drive—blue of all

Gilroy the garlic's
leaving us for China
to be creative
is to be in a state

where truth can come into
        being garlic oil
black so black
or white so white
or bird in flight

I drive damn I love it
past Morgan Hill
Caribbean Blue, Kings
Deep blue
and Cerulean
buttered in the belly
of San Jose I'm Naples and Sandstone
other fleshtone Flintstones that
that don't quite fit

Light to dark
warm to cool
color language
San Francisco
codes I miss
my city the birthplace
almost born to play

Here overnight
Seventeen stories above Japantown, my parents
crème de la crème
independent care retirement
but it's too still
chill Veneda Grey
Made from lime

twelve hosts of espresso
twist foghorn
tuxedo pavement
shadow junkies slumped
drip and hunk

City Lights, Cody's
Keplers then back to San Luis
drive and drive and drive

Bearing witness
KPFK out of Berkeley, probably
for the art of another twenty-five hour day

Faster Than Beauty

Jean Cocteau, born this day, 1889

Film makes possible
living an hour

instead of narrating it.

Michelangelo: the Sistine Chapel
a candle wired to his head.

Muses are preying mantises

a train
Destination: death.

Faster than beauty. Run faster!

As if turning your back
on it.

Countless Cinemas

with thanks to Donald S Lopez Jr.

The yogacara speak
of a form of consciousness

where all the seeds
of past deeds
are deposited.

One by one these seeds
come to fruition
simultaneously

creating a person
and a private world.

A universe of closet-sized cinemas
each occupied by a single person

eternally viewing a different film.

Everything is of the nature of consciousness.
The product of one's own projections.

Ignorance and suffering
believe the yogacara
result from feeling
the movie to be real.

Steiglitz, Skyscrapers, & The Met
11/11/11 Manhattan

They curve to meet the clouds,
the empire states, the obelisks,
the sand boxes, the shakers,
the little sisters,
the xylophones,
the saltines,
the tin peckers,

the bird seed avenue.

One need not be gravy to see this.
One need not be fine grained snow.

Bulls of Bordeux, Lake of Zug,
the only good Raphael bronze,
tears for you, wet plate collodion,
a showroom of laughing
atmospheres, the commode in red
damask. Monet.

They curve to meet steamfitter astrolabes,
the lipstick of Cecil DeMille.

They say, here because I'm smart enough
to get the best of you.
To be as pretty as possible
for destiny.

The Fang people don't worship Thor Heyerdahl.
Balzac's death mask a Maori feather box.

They curve cloud perfect
white marble
periods of
sarcophagi
millions of ibises sorted
through Egyptian mail

In the Namibian lion killed by Hercules,
in the pistol of Charles the Fifth,

the empire states, the obelisks.
a taut
reticulated skin pore
messenger

lunching.
At his lens.

Yellow Leaves & Mattresses
to Dona

The Indians called it hard climb. Tehachapi. Town where your
mother lived.

Months after your brother bled out, died hemorrhaging his brother-
in-law rakes the room.
First I raked bloody t-shirts off the mattress   Which had grown
ground beef
Oh Henry wrappers, computer keyboard, ripped jean
patch cords Silver orange wing Of a Cal Trans vest.
One *Little House on the Prairie* VHS.

Death by six pack Mostly. Blood crusted
Two foot liver Puddled By the door.
Brown broken Wine green mold walls.
Black panties like a mamba from the corner.
Seemingly somehow alive.

We blessed his ashes. Tossed his ashes.
Swung the little tin around.

Steel bridge Cold Springs Canyon
San Marcos Pass.

It seemed Chumash. 'Cause you guys are Chumash
I liked my brother-in-law. He was forty-five.

ACKNOWLEDGMENTS

With bottomless thanks to my father and son, to L. F. for your non-poetic catechism, to Tyler and Greg, for their forbearance/commitment/support, to Arthur and Gracie for the arcane and the original and to all those, living and dead, whose shoulders I falter upon.

Grateful acknowledgement is made to the following publications in which a number of these poems originally appeared: *An Eye For An Eye Makes The Whole World Blind: Poets On 9/11*, *ArtLife*, *Art Rag*, *ASKEW*, *Cafe Solo*, *Chiron Review*, *Coffeehouse Poet's Quarterly*, *Convolvus*, *Crack*, *The Forum: California Community Colleges*, *Enizagam*, *HopeDance*, *if/when*, *The LA Weekly*, *Maintenant: A Journal of Contemporary Dada Writing and Art*, *PoetryBay*, *Poetry Flash*, *Prism Review*, *Rivertalk*, *San Gabriel Valley Poetry Quarterly*, *Solo Novo*, *Sometimes in the Open*, *The Southern California Anthology*, *Tool Belted Liars*.

REFERENCES

Some of the poems in *Countless Cinemas* were inspired by or borrowed language from other original sources, some of which could not be tracked down, but are nonetheless noted. (Borrowed material was done so sans mal intent!)

POEMS & SOURCES

"Daylight Savings Time / de Kooning"
William de Kooning: Artist. Dir Robert Snyder. Mystic Fire Video. 1995. DVD.

"Neck Surgery Summer Exercise Program"
Based on a handout from the doctor who performed my spinal surgery 15 years ago. The original handout is long gone.

"New Cathedrals"
Mary Gibbs, "If You Want to Humble an Empire," *Time Magazine*, September 14, 2001.

"The Man Ray Story"
Man Ray: Prophet of the Avant-Garde (American Masters. PBS). Dir Mel Stuart. Winstar RV & Video. 1998. DVD.

"No End"
Inspired by an ancient article in the *LA Times*.

"I Would Have Taken a Cleaver"
Inspired by a 15- to 20-year old article in *The New Yorker*.

"Faster Than Beauty"
PROFILE OF A WRITER Jean Cocteau: Autobiography of an Unknown. Dir Edgardo Cozarinsky. Antenne 2 L'Institut National de l'Audiovisuel, J.C. Productions. Ministry of Culture, Paris, France. 1983. VHS.

"Countless Cinemas"
Donald Lopez, *The Story of Buddhism* (San Francisco: Harper & Row, 2001).

ABOUT THE AUTHOR

A three-time $17,000 California Arts
Council grant recipient, Michael
McLaughlin has worked for 25 years
as an artist-in-residence at Atascadero
State Hospital, a maximum security
forensic facility, as a Contract Artist
with the California Department of
Corrections, with California Youth
Authority, and as San Luis Obispo
County Area Coordinator for
California Poets in the Schools.

Photo by Gracie Malley

A graduate of the University of
Southern California's Master of
Professional Writing program and founding editor of its literary
journal, *The Southern California Anthology*, McLaughlin has
written two novels, *Western People Show Their Faces* and *Gang of
One*, and two chapbooks of poetry, *Ped Xing* and *The Upholstery
of Heaven*. His poetry and prose have appeared in numerous
publications.

Originally from San Francisco, California, McLaughlin lives
on California's Central Coast with his brilliant and beautiful
wife. Selected Poet Laureate of San Luis Obispo County in 2003,
McLaughlin runs the Central Coast's *Live from the CORE* poetry/
performance series and is an Artist in Residence at Pleasant Valley
State Prison in Coalinga, California.

THIS BOOK IS ONE OF THE MANY AVAILABLE
FROM UNIVERSITY OF HELL PRESS. DO YOU
HAVE THEM ALL?

by Tyler Atwood
an electric sheep jumps to greener pasture

by John W Barrios
Here Comes the New Joy

by Eirean Bradley
the I in team
the little BIG book of Go Kill Yourself

by Calvero
someday i'm going to marry Katy Perry
i want love so great it makes Nicholas Sparks cream in his pants

by Leah Noble Davidson
Poetic Scientifica
Door

by Rory Douglas
The Most Fun You'll Have at a Cage Fight

by Brian S. Ellis
American Dust Revisited
Often Go Awry

by Greg Gerding
The Burning Album of Lame
Venue Voyeurisms: Bars of San Diego
Loser Makes Good: Selected Poems 1994
Piss Artist: Selected Poems 1995-1999
The Idiot Parade: Selected Poems 2000-2005

by Lauren Gilmore
Outdancing the Universe

by Robert Duncan Gray
Immaculate/The Rhododendron and Camellia Year Book (1966)

by Joseph Edwin Haeger
Learn to Swim

by Lindsey Kugler
HERE.

by Wryly T. McCutchen
My Ugly and Other Love Snarls

by Johnny No Bueno
We Were Warriors

by A.M. O'Malley
Expecting Something Else

by Stephen M. Park
High & Dry
The Grass is Greener

by Christine Rice
Swarm Theory

by Michael N. Thompson
A Murder of Crows

by Sarah Xerta
Nothing to Do with Me

UNIVERSITY OF HELL PRESS

Denting the world with words,
one incendiary book at a time.

CPSIA information can be obtained
at www.ICGtesting.com
Printed in the USA
FSHW020852120719
59843FS